BUILDI S
BAYKO AND OTHER SYSTEMS

Brian Salter

SHIRE PUBLICATIONS

Published by Shire Publications Ltd.
PO Box 883, Oxford, OX1 9PL, UK
PO Box 3985, New York, NY 10185-3985, USA
Email: shire@shirebooks.co.uk   www.shirebooks.co.uk
© 2011 Brian Salter.

First published 2011.
Transferred to digital print on demand 2015.

Every attempt has been made by the Publishers to secure the appropriate permissions for materials reproduced in this book. If there has been any oversight we will be happy to rectify the situation and a written submission should be made to the Publishers.

A CIP catalogue record for this book is available from the British Library.

Shire Library no. 616.   ISBN-13: 978 0 74780 815 2

Brian Salter has asserted his right under the Copyright, Designs and Patents Act, 1988, to be identified as the author of this book.

Designed by Tony Truscott Designs, Sussex, UK
Typeset in Perpetua and Gill Sans.
Printed and bound by PrintOnDemand-Worldwide.com, Peterborough, UK

COVER IMAGE
Three of the four most fondly remembered British Building toy brands, all of which first appeared between the two world wars. All were very popular again in the late 1940s and 1950s, before succumbing to the onslaught of plastic.

TITLE PAGE IMAGE
Very familiar Bayko, but with grey bases, and even grey bay window covers. The addition of a chain-topped wall by the builder is also period-correct, actually inspired by the instruction manual front cover (Figure by Owen Miniatures, with a Corgi Classics Ford Popular).

CONTENTS PAGE IMAGE
Two separate Chad Valley systems with the same structural members. They were good value for money and had good play value, especially when combined. Large combination sets sold particularly well.

ACKNOWLEDGEMENTS
Thanks are due to the many members of the Bayko Collectors' Club who, over the years, have provided a constant stream of material and information for display and recording at club meetings. Particularly noteworthy in their own specialities have been Peter Bradley (Bayko), Gary Birch (Lott's Bricks), Malcolm Hanson (Minibrix), and Robin Throp (Airfix), whilst Jackie Briton has answered many questions generally and contributed particularly to the first chapter in her own inimitable way.

Various other collectors have also loaned items for photography, including contemporary vehicles and figures to help set the scene.

Photography by Roger Wynn Studios.

CONTENTS

EARLY VARIETY

EXACTLY when children started using small blocks as a building toy is lost in the mists of time. Wooden offcuts, perhaps reduced to a regular size by a local craftsman, may have been a prized possession, but for the purposes of this book the story of building toys begins with the onset of industrialisation. The ability of at least a small section of the population to afford such a luxury as a manufactured toy is paramount.

More than six hundred manufactured systems of building toy have been identified worldwide. Many of these make use of some form of interlocking for at least a basic rigidity, but systems relying on nothing more than friction and gravity lasted much longer than might be expected. Wooden and stone pieces, representing not just bricks but columns and arches, were available from various manufacturers by the late nineteenth century. One such system, Anchor Blocks, even came to dominate the whole building-toy market for an extended period. Nonetheless, some form of interlocking is desirable, and developments aimed at achieving this seem to go just as far back. One basic method, which could be described as 'American log cabin', had machine-produced notched and grooved wooden pieces fitting securely together.

As the market slowly but surely expanded in the twentieth century, there was no lack of ingenuity. Thus far, building toys had been intended for constructing, and reconstructing, toy buildings, but the first major development of the new century was an engineering toy, Meccano. Produced from very humble origins by Frank Hornby, it worked, and it worked very well owing to strict manufacturing standards. It also represents one of the first uses of metal in constructional toys, and it soon had competitors.

Another of these was Kliptiko, invented by William Bailey Ltd of Birmingham in 1913. It was, and still is, referred to as 'the poor man's Meccano'. The system used the company's expertise in sheet-metal fabrication and relied on interlocking steel tubes.

Out of the same factory came Wenebrik, 'an instructive architectural toy', patented in 1916. Every Wenebrik component was either painted or plated sheet steel, the slotting together of which required no small amount

Opposite:
Even the box of the Goodtoy set is steel. Many of the construction ideas shown are merely façades, and to this end some interior panels are provided. Full buildings above a single storey can prove to be very frustrating.

5

The start of a Wenebrik house on its 'gold'-plated bases. Included are a small stack of green roof tiles, and two different pieces of guttering. Assembly was not without its dangers, despite very careful manufacture.

of pressure. Despite the risk of injury, the roof was built up with separate tiles, and there was even a complete roof gutter system, a feature only ever found on a handful of other systems anywhere. Despite being in at the start of the British building-toy industry, the firm decided in the early 1930s to concentrate on its main business.

There were no parts common to both Kliptiko and Wenebrik. There were no architectural parts in the Meccano system, though buildings could be constructed and even received some publicity. Another competitor, in the early 1930s, saw things differently. Arkirecto, by the firm of the same name, used a metal framework of 'girders, joiners and stanchions'. Their architectural 'A' sets had lithographed cladding panels, instead of gears, pulleys and wheels. The effect, particularly of the multi-storey buildings, as shown by their artwork, was very satisfactory. All sets contained a small wooden hammer to help with construction.

This girder and panel method was to reappear some twenty years later, but there are two other metal systems to be mentioned. Meccano wished to enter this market, so in 1934 they introduced Dinky Builder. This was something completely different, aimed at the younger builder. Its flat

Edwardian-style presentation for this Wenebrik tinplate set. The artwork of the various makes is a social history study in itself. The clothing of the young builders changes, as do the activities of the ladies, where they are present at all.

enamelled plates, held together at their curved interlocking edges by metal rods, were equally suitable for dolls' house furniture or as part of simple wheeled contraptions. Providing wheels was a thoughtful act that was to be repeated many years into the future to broaden the appeal of other building sets.

Somewhat later in date, but probably not preceding the Second World War, the Goodtoy Magnetic Construction Set adds variety. Its shallow steel tray acts both as box and building base, to which numerous small iron magnets are attracted. In their turn, some very colourful printed tin panels are brought into contact and held fairly firmly. Strangely, there are two heights of wall panel and door, therefore two scales in one box. Even more unusually, some panels are designed as interiors.

The unavailability of German-made products from 1914 onwards may have encouraged Wenebrik, Dometo and, certainly, Lott's. Although wood was a constituent of many systems worldwide, its use in this period in the United Kingdom was limited. Dometo, made by the Irish Toy Industry of Belfast, relied on wood. It had relatively simple shapes for bricks and separate roof tiles, but complex machining for corners and gutter cornices. Its large

With Arkirecto, the same girder framework formed the basis of both engineering and architectural projects. This could be the first attempt at true miniature multi-storey construction. Years later, the method would reappear spectacularly.

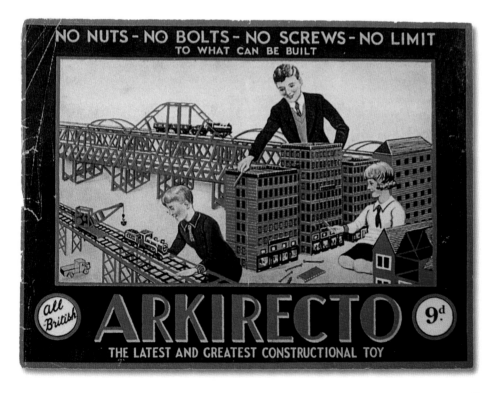

Right: From the outset Dinky Builder tried to be all things to all men – and boys and girls. This late-1934 introductory advertisement says it all – architecture, transport and domestic subjects are all shown. Later, many other building systems tried similar multi-tasking techniques.

Above: At first Dinky Builder did not include doors and windows. Later they were printed on. This may be the only system where a single-storey house is not possible, or where a fully edged front path can be added.

Right: Dometo, from Belfast, entirely in wood and a great improvement on plain blocks. The roof tiles are simple to use and survive well.

size and easy assembly made it an attractive proposition and a great step forward from the simple wooden block.

A few years later the Dometo name was transferred to something outwardly similar, manufactured by the Improved Solidite Company of Wandsworth, London. The material was very different, though – a cast composition that can be accurately moulded to quite intricate shapes. It was an early use of peg and

Dometo, from Wandsworth, in moulded composition, and completely different from its Irish forebear. The heavy roof needed support, which worked quite well, but the tiles were very easily damaged.

socket location on the bricks, some of which even included a slot to take roof rafters to support the heavy tiles. The roofs must have been striking when new but the doors and windows were somewhat crude.

A much harder composition, in effect artificial stone, was used from the same period onwards by Lott's Bricks. Their simplicity and quality, plus the fact that they were British, made them a winner from the start. A completely different concept, but with a similar raw material, was Brickplayer. Tiny miniature bricks had to be actually cemented together, and production started at about the same time as the Second World War.

Two systems, Buildo and Samlo, made good use of the most basic of materials, cardboard. Alldays of Birmingham introduced Buildo around 1915, featuring grand ornamental half-timbered designs. Their Edwardian style of box artwork could be considered the most attractive packaging of all building toys, and they promised that the contents would 'provide comment and instruction in the design and form of our unrivalled English homes'. Flat-packed sections were held together with special tiny split pins and could be given extra support inside by strategically placed metal strips. Complex buildings could be achieved, with roof styles and chimneys to match. One of the advantages of card was that individual sections were not only cheap to produce,

Irish Dometo (left) had doors and windows in the larger sets, but always a very neat roof ridge line. The English version's brickwork (right) was more convincing, the finished roof much less so.

9

COUNTRY COTTAGES.—SET A.

but also cheap to design. A substantial amount, both in variety and quality, could be arranged in a shallow box and would expand remarkably on building.

Samlo, manufactured by J. Waddington of Leeds, well-known for their card games, had the same advantages. Construction was by the tab and slot method, much as used in tinplate toys, but it was now 1936, and the architecture was very different. The card is textured to represent a rendered surface, whilst all roofs, floors, doors and windows are available both in orange or bright light green. Samlo can form curves and flat roofs to match, in a severe 1930s style. The largest set, set E, came in a plain red three-drawer cabinet (in contrast to the gorgeous gaudy box illustration of lesser assortments) and boasted no less than 697 pieces. It could cover quite a lot of table-top and is surprisingly rigid, as long as it has not been used too much previously.

The next material to be tried was rubber. In 1935 the Premo Rubber Company of Petersfield, Hampshire, introduced Minibrix. This was the first truly simple interlocking system, featuring a child-friendly push-fit that eventually virtually ousted all others. Minibrix also ran a separate half-timbered Tudor range, as did Lott's.

Not a chocolate box but a children's toy: another system from the flurry of activity around 1913 onwards. It could not be more English in appeal. Unlike most fanciful box artwork, the contents of the larger sets at least had the potential to match the vision.

This smaller Buildo set is too fragile now to rise up again. Tiny split pins pass through holes in overlapping card sections, the pin heads serving to replicate the wooden dowels or pegs used in real timber joints.

Also during the 1930s building-toy rivalry a completely new material appeared – bakelite, commonly credited as the first commercially available plastic. It became closely associated with the first plastic toy, Bayko, in 1934. Its system of structural uprights with panels slotted between was in due course mimicked in wood and card around 1939 by Fabro of Liverpool, which claimed to be aimed at younger children, but Bayko was not that unsuitable in this respect and was very well established. With its long production life and the consequent inevitable changes, Bayko had a very colourful history and is now the unchallenged brand leader of vintage and classic building sets.

Minibrix, Bayko, Lott's Bricks and Brickplayer survived the Second World War to become the 'big four' building toys of the 1950s. Almost everybody of the right age seems to remember at least one of them, so each will be looked at in more detail.

Unused Samlo card sections with both 1930s suntrap windows. The plain cream textured finish and the ability to form curves put this system, architecturally at least, ahead of all others at the time.

11

LOTT'S BRICKS

THE MOST BASIC, and earliest, of the four best-known building toys is Lott's Bricks. The system had its origins in 1882, in Thuringia in Germany, with the introduction of Richter's Anchor Blocks. Through good marketing and good quality, Richter's eventually had around a thousand different stone shapes, arranged into six hundred different sets. Naturally their design reflected German architecture of the period, mainly 1870s baroque. The blocks were imported into Britain and they were very popular.

As a British manufactured toy, Lott's Bricks are a product of war. After the outbreak of the First World War the British government severed all trading links with Germany and encouraged the home manufacture of goods no longer obtainable as a result. Those children lucky enough to possess commercially produced toys would quickly notice the difference as Germany was the main source of these toys. It has been written elsewhere that 'E. A. Lott was granted Richter's [London] factory as part of the war reparations in 1919', but there never was a factory to take over. Recent research has discovered that there was no connection between the two firms, other than the transfer of an idea.

The idea came to Ernest Lott well before the war as he observed his children playing with Anchor Blocks, and he became convinced there would be a market for a simpler English-styled version. So serious was he that experiments on ways of making the bricks were started. By 1915 Lott was looking for a job, had the knowledge and knew the market. There was also the possibility of government assistance. At the age of forty-one, therefore, he moved his family to Bushey, near Watford, and began trading as the Homeland Toy Company, but the name was soon changed to the Granitine Block Company when he became convinced that toy bricks were the way forward. A local quarry supplied one of the main ingredients, chalk, and another, marble dust, was a by-product of a different quarry supplying monumental masons. With the technical problems nearly solved, Lott wisely sought expert help with design and contacted Arnold Mitchell, a local architect based in Harrow. Well-known as a purveyor of superior suburban

Opposite: Suitable colours extended the appeal of many building systems to the youngest members of the household. Splinters permitting, this largest of the 1930s Lott's Kindergarten sets should provide hours of fun. With no doors or windows, the whole effect harks back to earlier years.

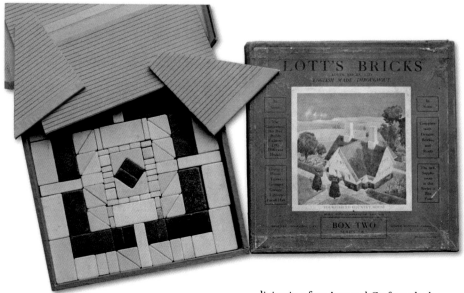

In Lott's early years black bricks accompanied white, and box illustrations and contents were designed around a particular building. This is the Ideal Home competition house, the designer of which became responsible for all the early Lott's architectural development.

living in a free Arts and Crafts style, he was ideal to incorporate the necessary 'Englishness' into the designs. He had come into national prominence in 1908 when he won a competition to design a £500 house, organised by the *Daily Mail* to publicise their first Ideal Home Exhibition.

The results of their combined efforts, with Mitchell even doing the brick styles and box contents, was unveiled at the 1917 British Industries Fair, itself a wartime initiative. The February issue of the trade journal *Games and Toys* introduced Lott's Bricks as 'a new line which has been in preparation for a considerable time past', and continued in the mood of the time: 'we think this line, which is of British manufacture, will prove itself to be a far better thing than anything Richter evolved. Our readers were, of course, very familiar with the German production, and know what extremely crude and unsightly buildings they made.' By this time the company name had again been changed, now becoming Lott's Bricks Ltd.

Mitchell had designed a system based on a 1-inch cube and a mere eleven shapes, all to be used in conjunction with hinged cardboard roofs. Windows and doors were represented by the simple expedient of leaving gaps in the bricks. The selection of bricks in each box was originally designed around a particular model, but also to give a pleasing symmetrical layout when packed in the box. Each set thus stood on its own, but of course any or all could be combined. All but the smaller sets came in wooden cases with slide-out lids, and great care was taken with the design of the full-colour labels. The artist, J. A. Swan, seems to have aimed for something rather like early hand-

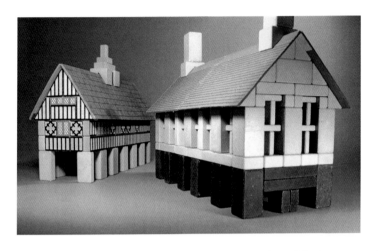

A very early Lott's market hall with square solid main blocks (foreground), said to be based on the one at Ross-on-Wye, Herefordshire. Behind is a much later and lighter Tudor Blocks version. Some form of market hall featured throughout the life of Lott's.

designed coloured postcards, but based on actual Lott's models. Surviving boxes in good condition are very attractive in their own right.

While the original styles remained much the same for most of the 1920s, in 1922 the first Tudor Blocks (not *Bricks*) set was introduced. This included hand-painted half-timbered designs, a labour-intensive and sometimes not very accurate operation. In 1926 Lott patented a raised or embossed design that could be roller-painted *en masse*, and the idea was soon to transform the whole range, but Tudor Blocks had it first in that same year. Though not the only building sets that can replicate half-timbering, they are even today thought of as the face of Lott's.

Additional fences, shrubs and trees have long been a Lott's feature. The earliest, at left, came in Garden Sets, but later styles were to be found within standard Lodomo and subsequent main boxes.

15

A scene with Lott's railway items. The large blocks on the wagon were intended as platform foundations, and the author has interpreted the grey diagonal pattern blocks as a form of wooden paling fence. (Wagon by Hornby, figures by Dinky, and track by Bing.)

Inside the lid of an early 1930s Lott's four-tray dealer cabinet. The railway items (price list, lower left group) and brown Tudor windows (lower right group) are now very hard to locate.

Despite the 1923 introduction of two sizes of Garden Set to embellish the buildings' surroundings, by Christmas 1927 there were difficulties. One West End store told a national newspaper reporter: 'Toys will share in the reductions in this store. Building bricks have not been in very great demand this season yet, so we are selling at a specially low price to clear this week.' Coincidentally, Ernest Lott was reducing his involvement in favour of his son, Arthur. Development and diversification would follow.

The all-new Lodomo building sets were available by Christmas 1929. As with the Tudor Blocks, gone were the 1-inch cubes, replaced by a uniform thickness of half an inch. The embossed design technique was logically extended to show doors, windows and brickwork. The new sets were perfectly timed and returned the product to popularity, setting the style for Lott's, with only minor adjustments, until their demise. The following year, further embossed designs were used to extend the architectural scope without disturbing the general scheme of things. Two Accessory Sets provided herringbone brickwork, diamond windows and a wooden-style door to be used with the Tudor sets, and another two had ecclesiastical-style doors and windows for the standard sets. A new stand-alone Railway Box included card platform sections and specially designed bricks.

At the start of the 1930s Lott's introduced a number of new products, one of which, the chemistry set, was to become a staple product of the company until their final days. In 1935 three Kindergarden Sets were brought out, with plain bricks in various colours, and in 1936 Buildec sets, featuring uncoloured bricks that needed to be coloured by the modeller, were introduced. The original windowless and doorless sets were abandoned with the introduction in 1936 of the new comprehensive Tudor Blocks sets,

For those of a religious inclination, two suitably equipped Lott's Accessory Sets were produced from around 1930. None of the two door or eight window styles was ever included in standard sets.

Lott's catered for OO scale from 1938 with Wonderbrix. This tiny cottage is a later one with some clear plastic windows, and the lady of the house is using a £1 coin instead of a wagon wheel for decoration. (Figures by Britains Lilliput.)

followed in 1938 by the New Series, a modernistic version of Lodomo, with gaudily coloured suntrap windows and doors. The Lodomo series, perhaps because of its more traditional styles and colours, remained alongside the New Series for many years.

Ever since the introduction of doors and windows, Lott's had been tied to approximately O gauge and scale. Previously, the relevant opening could have been left by the builder to any size, and hence scale, desired. In the 1930s OO gauge was beginning to be popular, and Lott's were quick to introduce their suitably sized Wonderbrix in 1938. Here a 'brick' became a complete wall section, some including embossed doors or windows on their otherwise plain

Based on early-1930s box artwork, these two farmyards show the subtle and often confused differences between the Lodomo series (foreground) and the later-1930s New Series. The latter attempted 1930s-style windows and had orange brickwork. (Figures by Britains.)

surfaces. The larger boxes could build a whole row of houses, ideal for a layout. A 1940 advertisement boasted of 'miniature bricks for grand bijou building schemes'.

After the war Lott's Bricks continued to do good business, but after a few years it became obvious that they were fighting a losing battle to maintain their position. Transparent plastic windows had been added to the New Series in 1949, and also to modified Wonderbrix units. Tudor Blocks remained a favourite, so much so that in the final years this was virtually the only type of building set advertised – the last time being in 1963.

The end of the old company came in 1968, with chemistry sets and supplies still doing a reasonable trade. Ernest Lott accepted an offer for the business, but the ensuing relocation to Barnstaple, Devon, to take advantage of government grants, was not ultimately successful. The family had retained the original factory site, and when this was cleared in 1979 Arthur Lott rescued a large accumulation of company records, which lay largely undisturbed for a quarter of a century.

Lott's at its most attractive: not quite as large as the box might suggest, but a very fine edifice that virtually became the face of Lott's in later years. It is instantly recognised by many.

After thirty years Lott's returned to a fairly similar style and size of box; even the artwork seems to belong to an earlier period. While it does have more colourful contents and a few plastic windows, comparisons are unavoidable.

19

BAYKO

T HE NAME 'Bayko' has not yet entered the language in the same way that
'Dinky' has – being used to identify all most any toy car – but it seems
to be heading that way. While the name is well remembered, it is the 1950s
colour scheme of red, white and green that most sticks in the memory. As
with Lott's, Bayko was manufactured by a company dedicated to its product,
but, unlike Lott's, the company never felt the need to diversify. The Plimpton
Engineering Company was formed by a trained engineer and clockmaker,
Charles Bird Plimpton (usually referred to as CB). The inclusion of
'Engineering' in the title was perceived to create the right impression of
quality, and to carry kudos.

Bakelite, an early plastic material, was developed in the early years of
the twentieth century by Dr Leo Baekeland in Belgium, and the name was
registered in 1907. The toy industry was not quick to adopt the new material,
but one of Plimpton's long illnesses gave him the opportunity to develop his
plans. The idea of vertical rods in perforated bases, between which building
elements were lowered, was not new. Brik-Tor, from the United States, used
tinplate elements, and Batiss from France had wooden ones, but the
similarities with Bayko are unmistakable. It has to be believed that CB had
some knowledge of them. His great leap forward was to replace tin and wood
with bakelite, with all its possibilities of shape and colour.

In November 1933 his provisional specification for 'An Improved
Constructional Building Toy' was lodged with the Patent Office, and by
Christmas 1934 the first Bayko Light Constructional Sets (numbered 1–5)
were available. The lower brick courses and architectural features were dark
brown (strangely called 'red' in the instructions), doors and windows a dull
dark olive green, roofs a deep maroon, and the whole was enlivened a little
by the near white of the rest of the bricks. There is often disbelief now by the
uninitiated that Bayko was ever anything but red, green and white, and
brighter and lighter bakelite colours were becoming possible, but the first
boxes were distinctly drab in colour. How the familiar arrangement of the
lower brick courses nearly always being 'red' was arrived at is often debated.

Opposite:
Bayko is famous
for its 'oak' parts,
making full use of
bakelite's colour
potential. A close
look also shows
orange mottling
on the olive-green
roof, and darker
patterns on the
very natural green
bases. This all
started with
Ornamental
Additions sets
in 1935 and
continued
throughout the
1930s, in one form
or another,
alongside standard
sets. (Modern
visitor by Owen
Miniatures; lead
tree by Britains.)

How Bayko started, in 1934, with various shades of brown, including chocolate and ginger, plus dark olive and deep maroon. Just an arch adds some architectural interest.

It was not a common feature in real life, although many public houses can be found with brown tiles from the windows down. There is a precedent, though, Lott's Bricks having done exactly the same, first with black stones, then after a few years with red ones.

Things soon brightened up, however. After a year, Plimpton added three Ornamental Additions Sets (termed A, B and C). Each included a couple of new parts and some others recoloured, but they were not comprehensive enough to model a building on their own. Full use was made of bakelite's ability to produce a mottled or marble effect and, when applied to the brown (i.e. 'red') parts, the result was attractively described as 'oak'. All of these were incorporated, in quantity, in a new 'super' set, number 6. This also boasted white doors and windows, 'oak' architectural features, and mottled green roofs. Sets in 'oak' were the only *full* sets, as opposed to accessory and conversion sets, to have all the bricks in one colour. 1935 was a very good year, and any resulting building was doubtless much admired then, as it is today.

The contrast to 'oak' – new parts in orange, and a new bay window. All came in new dedicated sets in 1938, and Bayko would never be quite the same again. (Modern cats by Omen Miniatures.)

In 1937 there was the first sight of the future – real red bricks and roofs, and a reasonably bright mid-green for doors and windows. Large brown bases were then standard. CB was not resting on his laurels, however, but his innovative mind was inventing again. The Ornamental sets were withdrawn and replaced in 1938 by four new ones (numbered 20–23). These, no longer termed 'Ornamental' as such, were the only sets ever not to have a standard or conventional roof included. Instead, there were domes, pinnacles and canopy covers, all in orange, plus variously shaped turret parts. The real innovation, though, was a curved bay window with brickwork to match. It became a permanent mainstay of the system.

Notwithstanding all this, the original sets of 1934–5 had remained basically unchanged, save for some colour alterations. A complete relaunch in 1939, called the New Series, incorporated much that had gone before. New, smaller bases and an attractive, more natural shade of mottled green provided much more scope in assembly. Most parts were available in more than one colour: for example, mid-green roofs and arches as an alternative to the more usual red. In addition, any set could be specially ordered in 'oak'.

Production ceased entirely at the end of 1941 but was quick to restart after the end of the war, albeit in a very limited way. A new introductory set O included a new four-part flat-packed roof, a development that was not fully exploited until well over a decade later. A number 3 set was not back on sale until 1947.

An immediate pre-war house from a period when most parts had alternative colours. The lighter green roof and arch are particularly notable. Bayko avoided landscape features but many builders must have added further embellishment, and they still do. (Lead gardening series by Britains.)

This almost brand-new small 1939–40 New Series set survived the war to do further service. Bayko, though not indestructible, does have a good survival rate, the bakelite parts themselves not rotting or corroding.

A 1940s window showcard, partly faded. There is a little artistic licence (where are the corner windows of the swimming pool pavilion?), and some of the parts shown were a long time in reappearing after the war.

Some colour experimentation was tried, but more serious proposals by CB resulted in a batch of new parts appearing in early 1949. Unfortunately, just weeks before they went on sale, he died after a prolonged struggle against tuberculosis. His wife, Margaret, continued the family presence, the next move being to introduce the large number 4 set with more of everything and all the new items. The early 1950s was probably the high point in the popularity of Bayko, and a number 4 was the aspiration of many children. Exports were paramount, and trade with the colonies and Commonwealth was buoyant, but the need and inspiration to develop further seem to have been lost. Plimptons could probably sell all they could make.

Bakelite nonetheless was becoming more expensive to produce and newer plastics were being perceived as more user-friendly. Competition and falling sales eventually dictated change, and so in 1958 the first new parts for nearly ten years started to appear. Most prominent was a pair of opening garage doors, made in polystyrene plastic. Most of the popular existing parts were retooled for this new material, and in the process the windows acquired glazing. To the casual observer, it has to be said, things appeared little changed and not even the box label was altered.

Further moves towards modernisation were probably afoot in 1959, but by the end of the year Margaret Plimpton had accepted an offer from Meccano Ltd for the company and product. Time and lives move on, and this must have seemed like a good way forward as Meccano had no significant product in the building-toy market. It is said that the last Plimpton sets left the original factory early in 1960. By the next Christmas a completely revamped Bayko was coming into the shops. Sets 11–14, in smart all-new shallow boxes, were almost entirely plastic,

BAYKO BUILDING SETS

A Fascinating Pastime for all Ages.
FACTORY NUMBER 803844
MADE IN GREAT BRITAIN

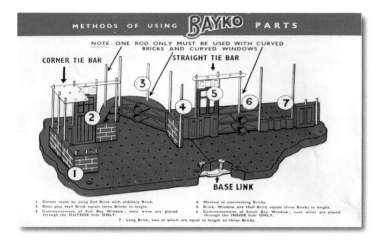

The toy world's most familiar explanatory drawing. It says all that the builder needs to know, and a lot of careful thought must have gone into its preparation.

had a much reduced range of parts, but boasted new colours and a completely re-engineered flat-pack roofing system.

Meccano is usually credited with all this, but in view of the short time scale, particularly with the roofs, it is the writer's belief that much must have already been in the pipeline before Meccano took over. What Meccano certainly did do was add a variety of new parts later in 1962. For the first

How Bayko is best remembered, even by those who never got to build the big house. It was on the front of even the smallest set and the early instruction book for most of the 1950s. The red, green and white scheme is surely engraved in quite a few minds.

25

Meccano's 1960 makeover: new colours and roofs, each standard set box carrying artwork relevant to the set's possibilities. A set 11, plus Accessory Outfits 11c and 12c, would exactly equal a set 13. Most brands operated a similar system of progression.

time ever they included an alternative roof *style* (not just colour or size) – pantiles. History repeated itself yet again, and all the new 1962 items became part of a new top-of-the-range set, number 15.

Sadly, this was the final high point. Yellow windows and doors, cream and red bricks, all under light green roofs or red pantiles, and even a shop front, were all very effective. Despite there being Bayko construction articles in 1963 *Meccano* magazines, the last advertisement appeared in February 1964. Bayko was still available until 1967, perhaps to service

The dormer window was a later addition of the Meccano era. It is worth comparing with the first ever Bayko from nearly thirty years earlier. Other than the colours, perhaps the biggest change is the garage. (Austin A105 and Humber Hawk by Dinky.)

26

existing customers and clear stocks. Competition with more modern systems was fierce, although none were particularly long-lasting or hugely successful, except for Lego, which was introduced into the United Kingdom the very year Meccano acquired Bayko.

Today Bayko's system of steel rods sticking upwards could never be marketed, but plenty of it seems to have survived. Throughout most of the product's life, the instruction book stated: 'Bayko sets are clean and hygienic; easily sterilised by placing in boiling water [later changed to 'diluted antiseptic']; ideal toys for children incapacitated by sickness and disease.'

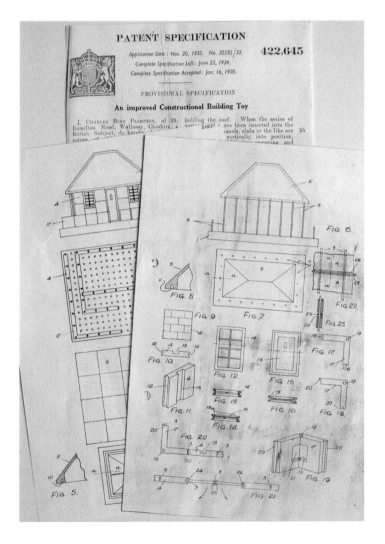

Doubtless most system inventors thought theirs was the best. The resulting patent application numbers appear with unfailing regularity. If successful in the market place, further developments often resulted in fresh applications. This typical example is Charles Plimpton's first one for Bayko, fully accepted a few months after his invention was launched.

MINIBRIX

JUST AS Bayko was looking like a success for its inventor, along came Minibrix, about as different a style of building set as it was possible to get. It is very important in our story, because it was the only building toy to use rubber as its main material, and because the system of assembly it employed is used almost universally today. There was no ground-breaking technology for its initial manufacture, as the ITS Rubber Company, formed in 1919 in Petersfield, Hampshire, was already well versed in the processes involved. Its founder, Arnold Levy, had been to the United States and seen the revolutionary processes used there in making rubber footwear. British production was started under licence, as a useful adjunct to his father's business of supplier to the shoe repair industry. ITS were the initials of the American firm's proprietors.

Arnold Levy and his American wife, Lena, had no children, but his brother, Moss, had nine. Perhaps Arnold had seen the Bild-o-Brix interlocking rubber bricks, a 1934 introduction from the United States, but it was Moss who asked:

> Why cannot we have a rubber Meccano? Here I am, paying out a fortune every month for toys of all sorts and kinds. Not only is it costly, but most of them are destructive. Even such toys as "X", which is very wonderful, scratch good furniture when the children decide to build on the table. Let us build something of rubber that will be acceptable to parents, educational, safe for children, and not destructive of the furniture.

Meccano in rubber sounds rather dubious, but Arnold came up with the idea of rubber bricks, with each small unit having protruding studs below and matching sockets above to interlock with the next course. The company needed a new product and so samples were produced. The advertising manager saw the potential, Minibrix was born, and the Premo Rubber Company was formed as a subsidiary to manufacture it.

An appointment was obtained with Selfridges' toy buyer, purely to appraise the system's prospects. The result was an immediate order, even

Opposite: Since the late 1940s the Minibrix Junior Set had contained bricks in four pastel shades. Rubber bricks are well suited, even for the youngest child, and the strength required to assemble them is a useful development aid. Today, though, some collectors find them hard to accept. (Plastic farmhand by Britains.)

This is how standard Minibrix is generally remembered. The builder has been fortunate to have a large rubber base on which to mount his interpretation of a small waterworks, complete with cottage and office, based on two separate set 4 buildings. There is even a hint of architectural grandeur. (Figures by Crescent.)

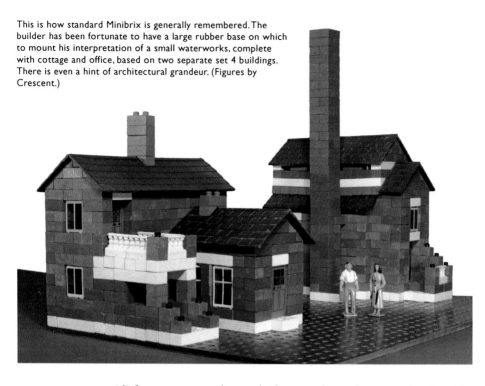

before prices were discussed. The same day, orders were also placed by Harrods and Hamleys and, with some reserved for Gamages, the first year's production was accounted for. A patent application was made in July 1935, just a month before the date on the first instruction book. The first display at Selfridges for the 1935 Christmas season included a Minibrix model of the shop's famous exterior.

This later 1930s box still uses artwork that dates back to Minibrix's first year, 1935. During assembly at the factory, great care was taken with an attractive layout, even with this fairly basic item which merely converts a main set 4 into a 5.

Things did not stand still, despite the sellout, or perhaps because of it. Extra parts were added in 1936, notably the balustrades and pillar sections, and the roofs were now single-piece moulded rubber instead of printed card. Heavy rubber baseplates were made available for sale separately in five sizes, making the construction much more secure and movable. Advertisements were now appearing in publications such as *Meccano* magazine and *Boy's Own* paper, and further large display models were produced – Buckingham Palace was an example that has a permanent place in Minibrix mythology.

Progress continued, and in early 1937 Tudor Minibrix appeared. By making almost all the bricks and lintels available in black as well as white, and with just a few new parts, the whole appearance was changed. Although Tudor Minibrix was packaged as separate sets in three sizes, the parts were fully interchangeable with the standard sets. New separate roof tiles, in four types with wooden purlins to add support, gave improved appearance and potential.

Top of the 1937 range was a new De Luxe Combination Set, containing, all in one box, the largest standard set (number 7), the largest Tudor set (number 3) and the largest baseplate (14 by 21 inches). By 1940 an even grander-sounding 'Imperial Cabinet' was available, but it actually contained only the standard number 6 and Tudor number 2 sets, but still the largest base. Also, empty De Luxe cabinets could be purchased to hold the builder's growing collection – an excellent idea.

Despite various proposals, the only further development before the Second World War was the introduction of a bright yellow box. The company also started its own dedicated club, the Minibuilders' Club. Membership was free, but members were

Instruction book exteriors from Minibrix were among the most attractive in the business. Both standard and Tudor series had their own books at first, here shown top and bottom. Later, both were combined in one volume, the earliest having a yellow cover. Most manufacturers built 'supermodels' for display and exhibition. The spectacular Buckingham Palace, 'built entirely of standard Minibrix', appeared on the back cover for many years.

This issue of *Games and Toys* tells us that Tudor Minibrix was the new line from Premo for 1937, and also that pillars, balustrades and rubber roofs were recent additions to the standard sets. Such trade advertising is now a very valuable reference source.

Right: The largest sets of some ranges came in wooden cabinets. This is Minibrix's largest and has a title signwritten by hand rather than a paper label.

Below: A Minibrix De Luxe cabinet, a combination of the largest standard and largest Tudor sets. The largest possible base is in the lid, and it seems to have come with both earlier and later editions of the universal combined instruction book.

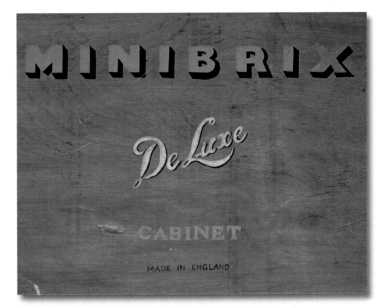

'expected to have a club badge' (costing one shilling) and would 'frequently receive the *Minibuilders Bulletin*, with advance information on new parts and developments'. There cannot have been a great deal to put in the *Bulletin* as the 1930s closed, and post-war developments would not be particularly newsworthy.

Any company with such specialised skills was quickly absorbed into the war effort, and it seems that it was not until 1947 that Minibrix was produced again. The company had manufactured everything from tank track treads to suspension systems for delicate instruments, and gained fame for pioneering the well-known commando-pattern moulded soles for boots.

Things returned to near normal, but with economies. The sets no longer had all their parts made up into façades or geometric designs for maximum appeal when the box was opened. The yellow box survived and became very familiar. Minibrix was selling well at home, and export markets, very important at the time, were, if anything, even better. The post-war boom led to some complacency at Premo, as often happened with manufacturers who just a decade earlier had been so innovative, and things did not improve after the death of Arnold Levy in 1955.

The yellow box is Minibrix's most familiar image. Later production economised by omitting such artistic layouts, but the trouble was taken to update the young builders' attire.

Most manufacturers had a starter set, but Minibrix had an even simpler Introductory Set as well. There is just a single tiny roof and one each of the revised design of door and window. As a bonus, a club badge was included, itself a later style.

In 1959 the remaining family interest was bought out by Sir Charles Colston, who had built up the Hoover organisation in the United Kingdom after the war. He had then set up his own 'white goods' firm, now best remembered for its dishwashers, and ITS would be able to supply his rubber mountings and hoses.

The Minibrix production methods were still highly labour-intensive, each brick needing to be hand-trimmed with scissors to remove 'flash' or 'spew'. Consequently other casting methods were tried, but none was entirely satisfactory. Tudor Minibrix was discontinued, along with separate roof tiles and rubber bases. Just four main sets were now offered, all of which came in cardboard tubes.

Despite this, an attempt was made to update with the introduction of twenty-two different small boxed packs marketed as Minibrix Extra. Six of these contained the parts for a specific small project such as a bus shelter, and four had selections of standard parts. Twelve, however, did contain something new, mainly items to embellish the outside and surroundings of a building. While the likes of flower beds, trees and sundials were hardly likely to revolutionise Minibrix, garage doors, balconies and further window and door variations were long overdue.

It came too late, though, and by the late 1960s there were just three sets, revised to include some of the plastic extra parts. All three were also available in 'rainbow' versions. The decline continued in the early 1970s and production had stopped altogether by 1976, but it had outlasted all the British competition. Today only the product remains to remind us of what had been Petersfield's largest employer, with a staff of over 250. ITS continued to produce other goods until 1987, when the factory was closed, the site subsequently being redeveloped. Somewhere, probably not far away, is the location where, in the later 1970s, all the remaining Minibrix stock was dumped from a skip. As rubber often survives quite well when buried, the site could now be a treasure trove for enthusiasts.

Minibrix was real building with bricks, suitably contrived for the youngest age group upwards. It was user and parent friendly, but a little expensive. Collectors now hold it in high regard for its unique properties, impressive appearance, and possibly the smell. Although a few samples have deteriorated to the point of being almost useless, some, even from the 1930s, look and feel as fresh as the day the girls cut off the 'spews', up to eight cuts per brick, at 2½d per hundred bricks.

In the early 1960s Minibrix sets were packed in cardboard tubes, a cost-effective, if not well-received idea. In addition, a series of Extra packs included some with new plastic accessory items, many of which were proportionately much too small.

BRICKPLAYER

BRICKPLAYER was the last of the 'big four' building sets to appear and is, after Bayko, probably the best remembered. It was produced by J. W. Spear & Sons Ltd of Enfield, who were generally well-known for indoor games and similar items.

Joseph W. Spier, born in 1832, had emigrated to the United States from Germany at the age of twenty, becoming an American citizen in 1860. Late in 1861, following the outbreak of the American Civil War, the family, now called Spear, moved back to Germany and soon found work in the same lines of business that are still associated with their name. In 1878 a company called J. W. Spear was formed in England as fancy goods importers, whilst the following year in Germany Joseph was the sole proprietor of his new manufacturing company. Despite some serious setbacks and the unfortunate death of the founder, the firm prospered under family control, having become J. W. Spear & Sons in 1884. While the original factory continued the production of toys and cards until it was destroyed in the Second World War, much of the production had been moved to England in 1932 as the influence of the Nazis became stronger.

Just how Spears came to develop Brickplayer is not known, but, being established in Britain in the reasonably optimistic 1930s, they must have been well aware of the building-toy potential. In particular, they might have taken a close look at the products of Gulliver Brick of east London, whose miniature bricks were very similar to the eventual Spears product. Gulliver is virtually unheard of now, and it is conceivable that Spears bought them out. We do not know, but the timing would fit.

Brickplayer reached the shops a few months before the first wartime Christmas, its initial *Meccano* magazine advertisement being in December 1939. There already had been artificial systems in stone, plastic and rubber, but now it was real bricks, real cement, a real trowel and real mess. Two sizes of kit were available, each also containing foundation plans, card doors and windows, and pre-cut roofs. Accurate results could doubtless be achieved with practice, but any attempt was very time-consuming, and it is hard to see

Opposite:
'Model No. 2
Siding Office' was
almost the smallest
in the Brickplayer
instruction book –
this is the earliest
incarnation. At left
is a waiting room
and shelter of
1950s materials.
The truck carries
Hornby wooden
bricks supplied
purely as a load,
but doubtless
some were used
for their (real)
intended purpose.
Similarity with the
Lott's railway
scene on page 16
is intended, with
accessories from
the same source.

Although the box style may be very familiar, this Brickplayer set is subtly different, with the earliest cardboard windows and doors evident. These had to be cut out from the very stiff card, but the pantile roofs were pre-cut and scored to fold neatly.

The two standard Brickplayer sets were supplied with roofs for twelve specific buildings, all of which, except a smaller station building, appeared on the manual's scenic cover. The three larger public buildings all have flat roofs.

now how any child would have the necessary patience. In all but the warmest and driest environments, setting was a slow process, as were the eventual soaking and thorough cleaning of the bricks if they were to be reused.

After perhaps just eighteen months on sale, other products had to take priority. When production resumed, or at least shortly afterwards, the doors and windows were replaced by cast metal ones that could be properly incorporated into the building process. Foundation plans were now true miniature blueprints. The advertisements heralded these as the 'vastly improved 1947 kits'. It was always possible to build to one's own design, of course, but plans and roofs were designed to make six or twelve (depending on kit size) particular buildings, not all of which could be built at one time. Railway subjects formed part of the regular repertoire as the kits were eminently suitable for O gauge. A signal box and two sizes of station were detailed, and suitable platform material was included in the regular sets.

For further variety, a more specialised Farm Kit was introduced in autumn 1953, more expensive than the largest standard set. Seven models were envisaged, but further bricks would be required if more than two were to be built together. Helpfully, a larger bricks pack was especially available to complete the rest, costing nearly as much money again. When one had completed all this, there was even a 5 foot by 3 foot green cloth and a layout diagram in the main kit to help set it all out just like the picture on the box. The rather rustic appearance of some attempts at Brickplayer is suited to farm subjects. Windows and doors were now plastic, and the standard sets had changed to the new material at about the same time as the Farm Kit arrived.

Almost exactly six years later, in 1959, the system had something of a makeover. More modern doors and windows gave a whole new style to

This Brickplayer dealer's tray has items in both plastic and metal, the latter being the cream bay windows and maroon doors at centre. Retailers could replenish stock by ordering separate items.

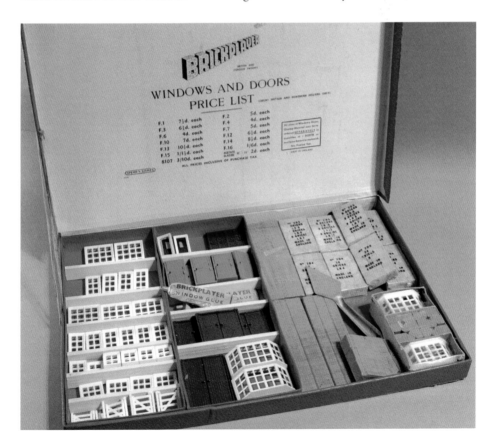

Contemporary Brickplayer, alongside shallower, flat roofs and paler-coloured bricks. Twelve new contemporary models, but with a subject choice very much as before, were 'architect designed for O gauge scale'. Unfortunately O gauge was no longer prospering.

Like many manufacturers, Spears ran competitions. In the early 1950s theirs was an annual event. Recognising the kit's limitations, they allowed a free hand with roofing materials and other embellishments as long as the main structure was Brickplayer. This was a valiant attempt to broaden its appeal and encourage sales of separate parts, and especially of packs of bricks. However, by the early 1960s only the Contemporary Brickplayer and accessories were being advertised.

It is amazing how well-remembered Brickplayer is today. Numerous kits turn up that have obviously been used, but whose bricks have then with great care all been scrubbed clean and replaced. By checking the roofs and other card sections, it is even possible to see what was built, and surprisingly the card signal-box steps are often unused. No parent could forget the operations involved, and there is a firm suspicion that many were more than mere onlookers. Perhaps the front of the farm booklet gives a clue – 'Footnote to fathers of children not old enough to build this farm. Why not build it yourself and give them a toy they will treasure for years?'

Brickplayer still has its following and, in place of the original flour and chalk 'cement', it seems that a stiff icing-sugar paste is a great substitute, which even cleans off nicely.

Historians adore contemporary advertisements, especially in magazines that carry a date. It is easy to learn of a contemporary bricklayer's arsenal of 1959 from the Meccano Magazine.

Contemporary roofs could be flat, slightly sloped at 10 degrees, or the modern version of traditional at 30 degrees (previously 45 degrees). New-style doors and windows are included, as are blister-style roof-lights. Obviously, 'real' bricklaying was a boy's job!

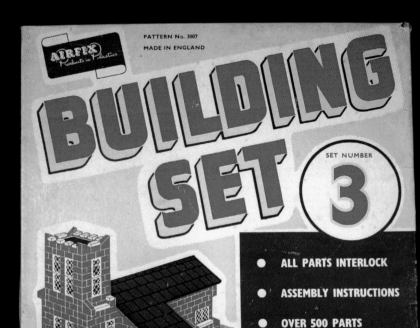

AIRFIX
Products in Plastics

PATTERN No. 3007

MADE IN ENGLAND

BUILDING SET 3

SET NUMBER

3

- ● ALL PARTS INTERLOCK
- ● ASSEMBLY INSTRUCTIONS
- ● OVER 500 PARTS

Including the realistic ROOFING TILES

PATTERN NO. 3901

building accessories

24 Pieces

FOR USE WITH THE
AIRFIX BUILDING SETS

Containing WINDOWS, DOORS, FENCES, GATES, ETC.

PATTERN NO. 39...

garage **Conversion set**

16 Pieces

MADE IN ENGLAND

FOR USE WITH THE
AIRFIX BUILDING SETS

Containing GARAGE DOORS, BAY WINDOWS, SHOP WINDOWS, & DOORS ETC.

POST-WAR PLASTIC

SINCE 1932 Hilary Page and some partners had been developing and selling traditional toys. Page was impressed with the ease of cleaning and attractive colours possible with plastics. Manufacture with the new material started in 1937 under his own Bri-Plax name, and soon included Interlocking Building Cubes. These were awarded a British patent in 1940. At the time it must have looked fairly inconsequential, and it does so even now in comparison with the systems already described in this book. Reference is often made to the idea being borrowed from Minibrix, and there are similarities, but it was, however, the beginning of the end for almost the entire building-toy industry as it was then.

Immediately after the war, plastic production resumed but now under the name 'Kiddicraft', which the partners had used earlier. Page has to be admired for his success at putting his observations of his children's play to good commercial use and as early as 1946 he contributed an article to the *Daily Graphic* Plastics Exhibition catalogue entitled 'Plastics as a Medium for Toys'. New to the range was a much smaller version of the cubes, the Self Locking Building Bricks, with sets first marketed in 1947. Bricks were square, hollow underneath with four studs on top, but there was also an eight-studded rectangular version. Only two other parts were in the line-up, a window and a door that fitted into slots in the bricks. These sets were advertised as 'Hilary Page's finest toy', and all items in the Kiddicraft range generally were well liked.

Meanwhile, with plastic coming into widespread use, Ole Kirk Christiansen purchased the first plastic injection-moulding machine in Denmark. It is said that it was demonstrated alongside samples of products, including some Kiddicraft bricks. Duly modified to metric dimensions and slightly altered, Christiansen's system was launched in 1949 and called the Automatic Binding Brick. Page was probably unaware that he had a very similar competitor – in Denmark at least. Neither system was particularly successful at first, but Christiansen introduced a more modern design, now called Lego, in 1958. Marketed as a system, it has been enormously successful.

Opposite:
An early Airfix set, the largest, but not large enough to build the church on the box. The typical Airfix bagged accessories have the later-style package design, and light green plastic has given way to white.

Morgan's toy shop was only a mile from the Kiddicraft factory, so local influence may explain Kiddicraft's appearance alongside Triang and Meccano on the shop sign. The shop closed in 1979, and the already historic sign was then painted over.

Model building competitions were a regular feature of some brands, but photographic competitions as such are uncommon. Although Kiddicraft entries featuring Building Bricks did not have to include children, the very simple system would lose much of its charm without them.

Lott's Bricks, Bayko, Minibrix and Brickplayer continued to battle it out, all the while introducing plastic where useful, but without compromising their established appeal. Little scope was perceived for new investment in yet another comprehensive system. However, during the 1950s and 1960s, three other well-known established brands entered the building-toy market. Following Kiddicraft's limited but well-respected success, their way forward was seen as the junior or starter sector of the market.

J. & L. Randall Ltd of Potters Bar, Hertfordshire, well-known for their Merit toys and games, were investing in plastic technology. They were early into the plastic model kit market, either repackaging or copying American kits, before producing their own to a very good standard. In 1954 they launched their Merit Brick Builder. They aimed fairly and squarely at building bricks, unlike Kiddicraft, whose instruction book also included such diverse subjects as an aircraft carrier and a piano. Because of Merit's use of soft 'unbreakable polythene', the first impression is very much of a toy aimed at the younger builder. Certainly the combination and interlocking of just single and double bricks to form the basic structure is still very like Kiddicraft, though of necessity to a slightly different design. Other features do set Merit apart, especially the probably unique

Kiddicraft Photographic Competition

Every month, Kiddicraft Limited award a PRIZE OF £5 for the best amateur or professional photograph of either a child playing with a Kiddicraft " Sensible " Toy or an original model built from Kiddicraft Self-Locking Building Bricks.

Whilst the winning entry is chosen principally for its composition and the interest shown by the child in the Toy, children need not appear in pictures of Kiddicraft Self-Locking Building Brick Models, where originality of design is the essential feature.

full corner picture windows. The sets also had two styles of doors, one with a curved top, a shape avoided by most manufacturers.

Although available only with white bricks and red features, and as sets merely packed in cardboard tubes, this is perhaps not such a junior system as it at first seems. The boy and girl on the artwork seem to be quite advanced, and when they reach the roofing stage, and need the three pages of cut and measure instructions at the rear of the booklet, they will need to feel quite grown-up. Hopefully the girl will not have recourse to her Merit nurse's outfit and first-aid items.

The Merit Brick Builder was distributed through wholesalers and had a good general exposure. It was probably available for four years or so. A similar time span applies to another product, at first glance very similar, also hanging on a well-known name. Airfix had been around as a plastics firm since 1939, manufacturing a wide range of domestic items. Ten years later they produced their first true model with numerous parts, the now famous Ferguson tractor. It led to the kit brand as we now know it. A leaflet, not later than early 1957, shows nine of the earliest aircraft kits and the full range of Airfix Building Sets.

There is no doubt, to the writer at least, that not only was the Airfix introduction inspired by the Merit product, but that Airfix had to take great care to be different. This was unimportant to the purchaser, but similarity to the Minibrix, Kiddicraft and Merit interlocking had to be avoided. Airfix came up with Lock-Bricks, which were assembled by sliding them together, this at times needing careful consideration of the order of construction. Instead of Merit's white and red, Airfix have red and light green, but resemblances include the two door types, free-standing garden gates and fences, coping stones, and cut-to-fit card roofs. Shortly afterwards, Airfix added individual roof tiles, and a larger set 3 to include them. An indication that the competition, Merit, had been seen off is given by a repackaging around 1958 and, most importantly, a change

In the United States Brick Builder was known as Block City and was almost identical to Merit's product. This, the smaller of the two sets, has the roof card as red pantiles, less suitable for use on flat roofs.

to white and red. A four-year minimum lifespan for Airfix Building Sets is likely, although some have given them much less. The complexities of the sliding Lock-Bricks are not well regarded today, but the simple roof tiles are hard to better for their basic purpose.

There was a gap of just a few years, and then in 1964 another attempt at the same market was made, by yet another big name, Triang. The bricks were bigger again, definitely for smaller hands, and the title 'Pennybrix' gives the thinking behind the price structure. It was manufactured by Minic Ltd, part of the Lines Group, and has to be given credit for a different marketing approach.

A mascot, Periwinkle Pennybrix, was given full billing on the boxes and instruction sheets, had his own full-colour story books in the sets, and generally tried to make himself useful. His miniature incarnation, about 2 inches tall, can be found in all but the most basic packs. These days he is often wrongly promoted to the rank of a lucky leprechaun from the Triang Spot-On Belfast factory in an effort to improve his stature (and saleability). He did have a car, though, a ready-made Austin Seven of sorts, and a railway train, both of which could run on the same tracking system. Two accomplices, much harder to find now, were usually associated only with tractor and post-van construction sets. 'Styled like a house brick' is a very apt description of these, but it does bring out the fact that after a year or two wheels and suitable mounts were added to the sets to give mobility. This all harks back to the thinking behind Meccano's Dinky Builder of the 1930s. Triang even

Brick Builder's colonial house, the largest suggestion in the instruction book. Every system has something special: note, therefore, the corner window, curved top door, and up-and-over garage door. (Gardener by Britains.)

Airfix's church, much as shown on the box, or as much as was possible. The use of light green was unusual and was relatively short-lived. (Figures by Britains.)

Another set is needed to complete Airfix's church. The roof tiles are just about the neatest and easiest to use in the business, but the slide-together bricks could be challenging. (Cart and carter by Britains.)

Right: Pennybrix in action. Just one car came in the Play Chest, but everything else did, and more. The roofs were even more versatile than this, quite something for a block system that was simple in the extreme.

Below: 'A Triang toy for the younger child' went the advertising, supported here by a shop display Periwinkle 21 inches high. The giant Play Chest is probably the last version of its type – the wooden superset – and may have been aimed at day-nursery use.

introduced a very large set with just about everything, including all three characters, all in a wooden cabinet.

This was a reasonably successful system with large modern bricks that Hilary Page would have approved of, but doubtless with reservations about the roofing. No separately tiled plastic roof is easy to assemble, but this one is as complex as any. Creditably however, and most unusually, both gable ends and hipped roofs could be planned for, and even full valleys, and corner valleys between two-way roofs and dormers. Parental assistance would probably have been required.

These four post-war plastic systems are all quite large in size to suit their purpose. Consequently, their larger scale is bigger even than the mainly O gauge compatible building toys already available. While all this was going on, OO gauge was steadily gaining in popularity, and smaller-scale plastic building sets became inevitable. Owing to the relatively small size of OO gauge, most ordinary smaller buildings could be provided complete as part of the railway, or as simple kits. With a kit, what you see is what you get, and Airfix exploited this very well as their kit business grew. But with the smaller scale, larger and larger buildings could be modelled and incorporated into the layout, particularly modern ones. It is for these that sets of parts again excel.

Just one large, basic unit, used in multiples, formed the basis of everything, and Periwinkle seemed to get everywhere! In a neat piece of marketing, extra bricks also came as a load in Triang's Jumbo truck range – Merton Abbey was just down the road from the factory, but the brick company is fictitious.

HIGH RISE

PLASTIC was making a great difference to the building-toy scene during the 1950s. There was no other material of choice for any new introduction. We have seen how it was particularly successful for younger children, but its light weight and strength gave it a clear advantage for the building of taller structures. For exhibition purposes at least, most major manufacturers were tempted to go beyond the bounds of what was possible at home and assemble spectacular larger buildings. In theory most systems could build upwards quite a long way, but the ultimate problem was stability. Usually some form of internal framework was resorted to. With the external walls being the main load-bearers, there was always going to be a height limit, real or miniature. The architect could design them stronger, but the model builder had fewer alternatives. The solution was the girder. A girder framework is comparatively light and strong for even quite lofty structures. The walls become little more than something to keep the draught out. So why should not toy building sets follow the same principle, and for good measure be able to build high straight out of the box.

Earlier, mention was made of Arkirecto, which, for its period, very effectively replicated a real building, girder frame first, then clad with panels. Twenty or so years later, in 1947, Albert Steiner, who with his two brothers had formed the firm of Kenner, was observing the construction of a new office building near his premises in Cincinnati. In 1957 they launched their suitably titled Girder and Panel Building Set.

Soon afterwards, the British brand-name Chad Valley was appearing on an otherwise identical product. Chad Valley had been around since the nineteenth century and was well respected. Careful examination of the small print on the box side reveals 'Made in England', so presumably Chad Valley had a duplicate set of moulds, as manufacture continued concurrently on both sides of the Atlantic. The system had great potential but was very simple, with just five main components – a foundation board, upright columns to peg into it and each other, horizontal girders to stretch between them, rectangular side panels, and square roof panels. Accurate moulding

Opposite:
A Jones KL10 crane assists, but there should be a tower crane somewhere. The sheer bulk of even a modest 1:42 scale Arkitex building is impressive but perhaps this limited its domestic appeal. (Crane and figures by Spot-On.)

This unsupported fifteen-storey structure is pure Chad Valley Girder and Panel, all as suggested in the ordinary set's planning book. Some parts and a highway have been added from Bridge and Roadways for effect, the whole epitomising the system's potential. (Coaches by Dinky.)

techniques allowed very fine dovetails to interlock at the top of the columns. In fact, they were too fine for the slightly brittle polystyrene plastic, which was later changed to more resilient polythene.

Panels were formed out of thin plastic sheet, with some variations in detail for particular purposes. The side panels were fitted on to pegs on the columns, but the risk of damage to the panel corners on removal was considerable. However, the result was quite sturdy, and an illustration caption boasts: 'Even tall buildings like this [fourteen storeys shown] are so rigid that they can be picked up by the foundations and carried about.'

The same structural components were also used for Bridge and Roadway (or Turnpike) Building Sets. Instead of panels, there were thin roadway sections, whilst the structural strength of the spans was enhanced by special

The panels of the Chad Valley sets were somewhat flimsy, but to fit into unusual corners (as by the recessed entrance) the instructions advocated cutting the corners. Almost unrestricted height could be built straight out of the box, or straight off the lorry. (Leyland lorry by Dinky.)

diagonal braces. All the parts, girder, panel, bridge and roadway, were brought together in large sets, complete even with motorising equipment that enabled some amazing projects. Although bestsellers, these sets are moving beyond the scope of this book, but the next development, Build-a-Home (and Subdivision) of 1963, is more relevant.

A girder frame in a ranch-style house from Chad Valley – a development of the easy-to-erect system, but with a hint of transatlantic style.

Eventually, somebody realised that the same structure could, with suitable cladding, be transformed into traditional buildings. All that was needed was an angled roof joist, new-style decoration of the wall panels, and new roof sections. It was still possible to build high, of course, but the general feeling is of low-rise ranch or colonial styles. The idea was to spread outwards, or, alternatively, a number of smaller properties might be built at a time, even from one set.

Such extensive building programmes, upwards or outwards, were possible only because these sets were in OO/HO railways scale. Girder and Panel must have been one of the earliest full systems to aim specifically at that market and was quite successful for around eight years in Britain, with further development until 1979 in the United States.

Perhaps its success, and even its shortcomings, encouraged Triang to think about something similar. In the late 1950s the owners of the biggest toy factory in the world were looking to move forward, and they also appear to have had money to invest in a new project. As the decade turned, many new products were in place, including Minic Ships and Harbours, Minic Motorways, TT-scale model railways, and Spot-On models. The last was a new brand which included model vehicles and roadways, dolls' house furniture, and Arkitex. Arkitex's main principles were remarkably similar to Girder and Panel. Alongside all these developments, Triang were introducing modern-style equipment for their OO railway, and a suitably scaled Arkitex could form the perfect backdrop.

A stronger joint between girders was a feature, and the fully modelled cladding panels came complete with clear windows, interchangeable coloured infills and opening doors. There were five sets in the main series, designated by the letters A to E. Particularly interesting was C, as it contained shop fronts, stairways and lighting units, while D permitted, not particularly successfully, the building of bridges and roadways. The best was E, with brickwork panels and balconies, which, rather late in Arkitex's day, made residential blocks possible. In 1963 four more sets, now termed 'Junior', were added. They were still lettered A to D, which can cause some confusion today.

Arkitex in 1:42 scale at left, and OO right. The sets 2 and B are virtually identical, and the boy, background and building are the same, but with the Spot-On crane or Triang Railway as a complement. The boy had to pose for fourteen box versions, all very similar, but all correct for the contents' scope and use.

For some strange reason OO/HO Arkitex was never marketed alongside Triang's railway system and in 1965 it seems to have been abandoned, but the following year, in the railways catalogue, we find 'R.589 Ultra Modern Station Set'. Although not named as such, it is Arkitex clearly enough.

In a parallel development, Triang produced another Arkitex in a larger size, virtually the old O gauge of the pre-war systems. Now, however, it was billed at 1:42 scale, and intended to go with their new, single-scale Spot-On vehicle and highway layout. Despite this, marketing failed miserably again. Even its base panels had been sized to fit in with the roadway sections, but it never appeared in a Spot-On catalogue.

The larger-scale Arkitex came in just the same five main set sizes as the OO/HO ones, and with similar contents, but now numbered 1 to 5. The constructed buildings in both sizes look very similar, but the larger scale allowed for some detailed differences. Location and fixing in some areas were more positive, but moving a built edifice was still a hazardous exercise.

In terms of development money spent, this has to be considered a failure. A look at the parts list for what are two separate products is revealing. Because of Triang's railway and road vehicle connections, it is tempting to say that Arkitex and Spot-On are much better appreciated

The back door of Arkitex in OO, the main entrance in 1:42. There are detail differences in the two systems in some areas. Eventually, four different colours were used on the interchangeable and reversible panels in the smaller scale, which points to its better sales. (Taxis by Matchbox and Spot-On.)

A later set, in both scales, had brick panels and balconies. The four-storey smaller-scale block is being extended, one of the stated advantages of Arkitex being that alterations were possible without major dismantling. (Vehicles by Minix.)

Three generations of Betta Bilda. The earliest is to the left, with the very attractive mid-1960s style (right) showing great potential for the upwardly mobile. The brand ended with a third scheme; just the Teeny Houses version is shown, but all had a similar artwork layout.

today. None of Triang's other *c.*1960 introductions stayed the course particularly well either, although the dolls' house furniture just survived to 1970.

The last system to be considered is the second from Airfix, completely different to their earlier larger-scale Building Set, as seen in the previous chapter. It was marketed as 'Betta Bilda' and reached the shops not long after Arkitex. As was the fashion by then, this was also attributed to OO/HO scale, but its small brick unit made it equally suitable for building a tiny cottage or a skyscraper. Various styles of plug-fit or snap-fit bricks have already been noted, dating back to the 1935 rubber Minibrix, but this is the most attractive of the small-scale systems.

It started as a relatively straightforward building toy with four different-sized sets. As with some other systems, there were no conversion sets to upgrade from one size to the next. A mere 350 pieces, including separate roof tiles, made up the smallest set, and 1,850 were in the largest. The second style of box artwork, from 1965 onwards, was very attractive in its suggestions for complete townscapes and high-rise cities.

A rethink from 1968 onwards brought considerable development, but with much less spectacular architectural artwork. Two Engineer Sets included wheels and beams to take Betta Bilda in new directions. There were even separate truck and rocket sets, and also, so as not to lose sight of its origins, three new starter sets marketed as 'Teeny Houses'.

All this late-1960s activity was presented as 'the integrated building system for all children'. Marketed as a 'system', Betta Bilda was enjoying considerable success, which was probably what prompted Lego to threaten legal action against Airfix on the grounds that Betta Bilda's very similar building bricks infringed their rights. According to the Airfix enthusiast and writer Arthur Ward, this threat quickly brought an end to Betta Bilda, which had lasted at least twice as long as Arkitex and was uncomplicated and versatile – just like Lego.

The fact that the Lego style of construction originates from the Premo Rubber Company of Petersfield seems not to be in dispute. Nor does it seem likely that Kiddicraft did not borrow some of the methodology, adapting to the plastics of post-war Britain. The bad luck for Britain, and this book, is that it was Denmark that hosted the further development.

The initial Lego sales were not too promising. There was resistance to plastics against the traditional wood and the locking ability was limited. After a further redesign, Lego as we know it only appeared in 1958 and arrived in Britain in 1960. A couple of years later the first wheels were added, surely the same thought process as the 1930s Dairy Builder. Although Lego is now a constructional toy where, given imagination and often some special parts, almost anything can be built, it still excels as a building toy.

But, to all intents and purposes, the British constructional toy for building buildings had run its course. Materials, fashions, and aspirations had changed greatly in the fifty-plus years since Ernest Lott launched his bricks. Many others followed, using every imaginable material, while worldwide not a few have utilised the Minibrix–Kiddicraft–Lego plug-and-socket idea. However, there was to be only one major survivor to emerge from our story of British building toys.

Betta Bilda's Teeny House at the front with its simplified roofing system (and tree). Behind are standard later issues, built small, using later alternative colours. (Vehicles, figures and accessories by Dublo Dinky Toys.)

COLLECTING

THE REASONS for collecting building toys are numerous, but nostalgia for a particular brand often kick-starts the passion. It is a visual memory at first, but soon methods, materials and long-forgotten projects and problems are recalled.

A good starting point is a well-used accumulation of the brand of choice, maybe still in the remains of its original packaging, perhaps from the local car-boot sale or a useful website. Some decision may have to be made: collecting it may be, but is it for building, to possess really good examples of the original product, or both? As ever, condition and rarity will usually dictate the price.

Many systems are still used as period scenic additions to vintage operating model railways. Some collect just by manufacturer – for instance, Meccano product collectors will only be interested in Bayko from 1960 onwards.

Generally though, membership of the Bayko Collectors' Club, which caters for all brands, will prove the best way of furthering the interest. The meetings are very informal and are usually held at Lane End Village Hall, near High Wycombe, Buckinghamshire, a few miles from Junctions 4 and 5 of the M40. All levels of skill are welcome, including none at all – it is the interest that counts.

For further information contact Robin Throp on 01727 826811 (robin.throp13@ virginmedia.com) or Gary Birch (*Bayko News* editor) on 01442 219183 (gary_birch@ btinternet.com).

Opposite:
Two club members combined a modern Meccano Big Ben kit (nearly 2 feet tall) with standard Bayko. The sculptured Gothic effect comes from using the bricks reverse side out. (vehicles by EFE and Minix.)

Below left:
Just a handful of prototypes of these three-piece balconies were manufactured around 1950, despite them being illustrated on most box tops and instruction booklet covers during the 1950s. These long-lost parts are now available as easily identifiable reproductions in modern materials. Tri-Ang's Arkitex also had parts that, though originally listed, are almost non-existent, and another enthusiast has remedied the situation there too.

In the year 2000 one club member decided to manufacture new design parts to fit the original Bayko system. Some elements, such as the door, had remained unchanged, except for colour, throughout the 30-plus years of production, and variety was long overdue.

Although this was a 1930s toy, what we would recognise as 1930s style would just have been too new then for a mass-market toy. but in the twenty-first century, from an enthusiast's viewpoint, such restrictions have gone. The first introductions, including an iconic sunray door, successfully led to a whole range of horizontally glazed sun-trap style windows. Diamond and herring-bone patterns can now also be enjoyed, as can corner quoins and oriel windows, from this continually expanding range.

Along with other members' replacement parts, and even seriously long replica rods, they are often on sale at club meetings. By joining (see previous page) one will automatically receive a free explanatory catalogue. Alternatively, four first-class stamps to PO Box 130, East Grinstead, West Sussex, RH19 3XQ will bring a copy, or to talk more try 01342 410502.

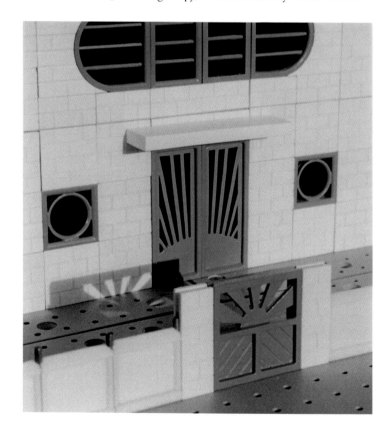

At long last, true 1930s style for a 1930s toy, marketed as 'Bayko 2000 Architectural Additions', and still covered by the original trademark. They have been developed in a way in which it is thought the founder, Charles Plimpton, would have approved.

FURTHER READING

The range of publications, both past and present, specifically covering
building toys is very limited. Brief mentions can turn up just about
anywhere, but most enthusiasts will have consulted the following:

Birch, Gary. *Lott's Bricks*. Bushey Museum Information 10, 2008. The result
of original archive research. A compact study of the company and its
products (see 'Places to Visit').

Hanson, Malcolm. *Bayko Then and Now*. Bayko Collectors' Club, 2009.
Mainly an updated version of a 1995 *Classic Toys* article. Good company
and product history.

Hanson, Malcolm. *Building Toys*. Gloucester City Council, 1990. Devised
to accompany a special exhibition at Gloucester Folk Museum. Includes
some engineering systems and kits.

Hanson, Malcolm. *Minibrix – The Unique Rubber Building Toy*. MW Models
Datafile 1, 1993. The standard work on the subject, comprehensive.

Harley, Basil. *Constructional Toys*. Shire, 1990. Good overview, including
engineering toys and Lego.

Bayko Club
members'
researches into
any relevant toy
company or
product regularly
appear in *Bayko
News*. It has
become a veritable
library of
information.

PLACES TO VISIT

Most museums relating to toys, models or childhood generally will have a building construction toy on display. The same will apply to any connected with vintage shops, advertising, household and domestic memorabilia. The boxes may even be open and occasionally a small building may be seen, but rarely is there more than just an example or two. Nevertheless, there are some destinations of special note, listed here. It is advisable to check the opening times, and where appropriate exhibit availability, before making a journey.

At the Brighton Toy and Model Museum's display of building toys is the splendid Richter exhibit, complete with clip-together bridge sections. The system is particularly interesting as the inspiration for Lott's Bricks.

Brighton Toy and Model Museum, 52–55 Trafalgar Street, Brighton BN1 4EB. Telephone: 01273 749494. Website: brightontoymuseum.co.uk. This seems to be the only place with a fairly comprehensive display. Two large full-height cabinets are dedicated to the main brands, quite a few of the smaller ones, and a number from further afield. Nearly all have built examples, many quite impressive. Most other toy and model collecting themes are also represented in strength.

Bushey Museum and Art Gallery, Rudolph Road, Bushey, Hertfordshire
WD23 3HW. Telephone: 020 8950 3233. A small display of Lott's
Bricks sets; also some unique factory memorabilia and artwork
available by arrangement.

Legoland, Windsor, Winkfield Road, Windsor, Berkshire, SL4 4AY.
Telephone: 0871 424 32280. Website: www.legoland.co.uk. Miniland is
a fascinating display of iconic and instantly recognisable British
buildings, together with other themed national landscaped areas. If you
have read this book, it is worth a visit for these alone. The rest of the
park could be a bonus for other members of your party.

Hertfordshire Archives and Local Studies, Register Officer Block, Pegs Lane,
County Hall, Hertford SG13 8EJ. Telephone: 01483 737333. Website:
www.hertsdirect.org. Custodians since 1979 of the Lott's company
archives (file D/ELo).

Museum of Liverpool. A major Bayko exhibit is planned to include the 16-
feet-high Empire State Building constructed by Bayko Club member
Leo Janssen. Progress and opening details can be followed on
www.liverpoolmuseums.org.uk

There is a hint of a 1930s cinema in this block, but Betta Bilda could have a go at most things, as suggested on the box lid. With everything to OO scale, it was a very useful and enjoyable product. (Vehicles by Dublo Dinky Toys.)

INDEX